> **RESTRICTED**
> The information given in this document is not to be communicated, either directly or indirectly, to the Press or to any person not autorized to recive it.

W.O. CODE NO.
926

MANUAL OF RECOVERY

(C) RECOVERY TECHNIQUE PART I

GENERAL INFORMATION AND TERRAIN

Issued by the Directorate of Mechanical Engineering

THE WAR OFFICE,
October 1944.

The Naval & Military Press Ltd

Published by

The Naval & Military Press Ltd
Unit 5 Riverside, Brambleside
Bellbrook Industrial Estate
Uckfield, East Sussex
TN22 1QQ England

Tel: +44 (0)1825 749494

www.naval-military-press.com
www.nmarchive.com

Front cover: The remains of Sherman tanks and carriers waiting to be broken up at a British vehicle dump in Normandy, 1 August 1944.

In reprinting in facsimile from the original, any imperfections are inevitably reproduced and the quality may fall short of modern type and cartographic standards.

CONTENTS

GENERAL INFORMATION

Sec.	Page
1. Elements of recovery	1
2. Training in subjects other than recovery	3
3. How a recovery task is initiated	5

TERRAIN

1. Influence of terrain on recovery work	11
2. Practical details of vehicular movement	12
3. Soil mechanics	15
4. Types of terrain:	
(a) Surface soils	19
(b) Subsoils	20
(c) Marshes, Bogs, Swamps and Jungle	27
(d) Beaches	32
(e) Snow and Ice	39

Permission to reproduce material from the following publications has been received:

"Geology of Soils and Substrata", by H. B. Woodward, F.R.S., F.G.S. (Messrs. Edward Arnold & Co.)—Extracts.

"Geology for Engineers", by Brig. Gen. R. F. Sorsbie, C.B., C.S.I., C.I.E. (Messrs. G. Bell & Sons Ltd.)—Extracts and Fig. 5.

"Phillips' Manual of Geology", Part I, edited by H. G. Seeley. (Messrs. Chas. Griffin & Co. Ltd.)—Fig. 2.

"Geology: Chemical, Physical & Stratigraphical", Vol. I, by Joseph Prestwich. (The Clarendon Press)—Fig. 11.

GENERAL INFORMATION

Section 1.—ELEMENTS OF RECOVERY

Definitions—" Recovery ", " Backloading ", " Evacuation "

In order to avoid any possibility of confusion, it has been found necessary to establish the precise meaning—in the military sense—of the principal terms used in Recovery and its ancillary operations.

These terms are as follows:

(i) **Recovery**

Recovery consists of one or more of the following operations carried out on a vehicle, gun or other heavy equipment, which has become immobilised as the result of enemy action, accident or mechanical failure:—

(a) The locating of the casualty.
(b) The rendering mobile of the casualty.
(c) The transference of the casualty—by towing or transporting—to a Recovery Post, Workshop, or other selected site.

(ii) **Backloading**

Backloading is the process of transferring, for the purpose of repair, a vehicle, gun or other heavy equipment, from a forward workshop to one further in the rear, *provided that no movement is involved through rail or road-head to Advanced Base or Base Workshops.*

(iii) **Evacuation**

Evacuation is the process of transferring, for the purpose of repair, a vehicle, gun or other heavy equipment, from a forward workshop in front of rail or road-head to Advanced Base or Base Workshops.

Recovery must never be confused with salvage. It will be clear from the definitions already given that the primary object of recovery is the facilitating, by every possible means, of the return of the casualty to operational use with the minimum of delay—whether this be achieved by immediate repair on the spot, or by repair subsequent to the transference of the casualty to some more convenient location.

Salvage, on the other hand, has for its primary object the collection of used or damaged military stores of every kind, for the purpose of " reducing to produce " the *materials* of which those stores are made.

Care Needed in Recovery

It is essential, during all recovery operations, to ensure that the casualty is removed speedily and without incurring any damage beyond that already inflicted by enemy action or other causes. Unnecessary damage occasioned during recovery merely adds to the burden of workshop personnel and delays still further the date on which the repaired vehicle, gun, etc., can again take its place in the battle. Carelessness in recovery operations inevitably helps the enemy, consequently crews must always bear in mind the need for safeguarding the casualty from damage.

The Importance of Experience in Recovery

Recovery problems can be segregated into distinct groups or categories, hence they lend themselves very readily to treatment along lines dictated by experience, or, in other words—the application of the principles of " recovery by comparison ".

In order successfully to follow this procedure, it is first necessary to have learnt—at some earlier date—the principles and practises used in the specific type of recovery involved; to note the salient features of the recovery task about to be commenced (thus ensuring that a correct basis of comparison is drawn); and finally, to apply this past experience without delay to the solution of the current problem.

The earlier lessons may be applied in various ways, not the least important of which is that of splitting up the selected example into its component parts and utilising the methods employed in one or more of them. Alternatively by building up an additional technique on some previously established practice, an unusual or particularly difficult problem may often be resolved with comparative ease.

Topographical and other features, weather conditions, the unlimited variety of damage which can be inflicted upon a casualty, etc., may prevent the application of typical procedure in every case; nevertheless, careful examination will show that in many instances the experience gained in handling one particular casualty can be applied either in whole or in part to the solution of another problem of similar type.

Requirements of Personnel

The rigours of recovery operations demand a high standard of physical fitness on the part of all personnel and it is the duty of each and every man to see that this requirement is fully maintained.

Personnel are selected for the specialised work of recovery in the light of their intelligence and ability to act quickly and decisively, and with close consideration of the mechanical knowledge.

The constant changes and improvements in recovery methods, together with the introduction of new equipment, render it necessary for every man to keep himself up to date, and to show the keenest interest in his own particular function as a member of a team or vehicle crew.

The team spirit demands co-operation between all the members of a crew; they must learn to work in close harmony with one another and at the same time to maintain that strict discipline without which efficient working and control is impossible. Any member of a recovery crew, therefore, who does not " pull his weight " and who tends in any way to disrupt the unity and team spirit of his fellows, will obviously be unsuitable for such a task, since he would not only imperil the lives of others but might easily jeopardise the success of the operation.

In brief, recovery personnel must keep fit, remain alert, be up to date with all technical developments, and above all, co-operate to the full with all members of their crew.

Use of R.A.S.C. Tank Transporters

Tank Transporter Companies, R.A.S.C., equipped with either heavy or light transporters, are allotted to Army, G.H.Q., or L. of C. The primary role of the Transporter Companies allotted to Army is a tactical one, namely, lifting the transporter of armoured formations so that in long moves track and tank wear is reduced to a minimum. When not so employed, however, Tank Transporter Companies under Army control may be allotted for the moving of reinforcement tanks forward to Tank Delivery Regiments, R.A.C., *or for the clearing of casualties from forward areas to rear areas for repair, thus augmenting the recovery facilities of R.E.M.E.*

It should be observed that the vehicles of Tank Transporter Companies, R.A.S.C., are now kitted with such recovery equipment as is necessary for them to effect simple recoveries of wheeled or tracked casualties within the limits of vehicle winch-rope-lengths from a hard road surface. Since tank transporter vehicles are primarily intended to travel on hard roads, they have little or no cross-country performance and therefore must not be expected to travel over soft terrain. The object of providing recovery equipment on such vehicles is to enable them *to assist R.E.M.E. recovery resources in an emergency.*

Section 2.—TRAINING IN SUBJECTS OTHER THAN RECOVERY

(a) General Training as a Soldier

The taining of personnel is not confined to technical work such as the operation of recovery vehicles and equipment. Primarily, each man must be an efficient soldier, having a good all-round knowledge of modern warfare in respect of weapons, fieldcraft, tactics, first-aid and anit-gas precautions. It is vital that at no time should the fighting efficiency of any man be relaxed.

(b) Training in Tactics

Casualties to be recovered will not always be in the rear of the fighting zone, and it is for this reason that recovery personnel must be trained in tactics. This will, in the majority of cases, involve evading contact with the enemy, who, it must be borne in mind, will be keenly interested in any recovery operations which may be in progress, and will attempt to interfere whenever he sees a chance of success.

The importance of evading the enemy must be kept well to the forefront in the minds of all personnel, since recovery vehicles and equipment—also the casualties—are valuable, not only to our own force but also to the enemy, for by their capture he not only ensures that casualties cannot be repaired and used against him, but what is even more serious, he may repair them himself (possibly by " cannibalisation "), and use them to increase his own stock of available equipment.

(c) Training in Ambushes, Booby Traps, Camouflage and Mines

The enemy may mine the vicinity of the casualty or he may attempt an ambush. The ambush may take the form of occupying the casualty (if an A.F.V.), virtually using it as a fort—possibly supported by additional camouflaged troops.

There is the strongest possibility that a casualty will be well protected by one or more booby traps. These are usually constructed with the highest degree of ingenuity, and are placed in such positions that their presence is most unlikely to be observed by any casual glance.

Approaches to casualties must be cautious and vanguarded by a scout, and for these reasons every man will be acquainted with fieldcraft and camouflage. Camouflage training should cover not only the act of effecting camouflage, but also how to *detect* camouflage.

Crews will not always be equipped with mine detectors, and they will therefore have to adopt extreme caution in areas where mines are suspected (or known), to have been laid. Special attention during training should be paid to the method of detecting and removing mines and observing booby traps.

(d) **Training in Map Reading**

Map reading plays an extremely important part in recovery. As in all military operations, map references are given when fixing the location of places, rendezvous points and—in recovery—the position of the casualty. Every man must therefore be conversant with map reading and the use of the compass; he must also be able to make cross-country journeys on routes devoid of signposts and with both natural and artificial features obliterated by enemy action.

Movements of this nature can only be accomplished satisfactorily by constant reference to a map, and by compass checking such courses as may be taken. Should the squad commander become a casualty, any other member of the crew must be capable of conducting the party both on the forward journey to the scene of the casualty, and throughout the return journey.

(e) **Training in First Aid**

Training of personnel to deal with human casualties is of the highest importance—first-aid instruction must be given to all and whilst it is not the normal function of recovery crews to deal with such stray casualties, in the absence of R.A.M.C. personnel they are expected to render whatever aid is possible, to be able to assist in removing an injured person from a casualty vehicle, and to make temporary provision for the comfort of injured persons.

Unless *returning* from a recovery operation, an injured person should not be taken aboard a recovery vehicle, and no time should be spent in locating R.A.M.C. personnel. A recovery vehicle should not be used as an ambulance unless absolutely necessary, mainly because of its unsuitability for this purpose (e.g., springing, stowage, etc.), and also because the carriage of badly wounded personnel must inevitably hamper the normal role of the vehicle. Preferably, send a message to the nearest Unit (by wireless or otherwise), reporting the location of an injured person.

(f) **Training in Burial Procedure**

Occasions will arise where the crew of a casualty vehicle is found by recovery personnel to be deceased. In order to cover such contingencies, therefore, recovery personnel must be acquainted, during training, with the procedure for burial of the dead. On no account must human remains be carried back to workshops or to base, since conditions of warfare are such that days may elapse before such a journey is completed; the transportation of a dead person in these circumstances is unhygienic, can serve no practical purpose, and presents the workshops staff with an extremely unpleasant task.

(g) **Training in Anti-gas**

Anti-gas training should be extensive, particular reference being made to the de-contamination of recovery vehicles, equipment and casualties. Here again, attention should be given to the possibility of booby traps; enclosed vehicles—eg., A.F.V.s—may prove, without warning, to have been contaminated with gas and should be dealt with cautiously.

All the subjects outlined in the preceding paragraphs " Training in subjects other than Recovery " are dealt with exhaustively in the appropriate Military Training Manuals; reference to them in these pages is made only with the object of guidance, and to impress on all personnel (whether engaged on technical or general duties), that its *military efficiency* is one of the criteria by which a recovery crew must ultimately be judjed.

Section 3.—HOW A RECOVERY TASK IS INITIATED

Upon an item of military equipment—whether vehicle or otherwise—becoming a casualty, the personnel of the Unit to which it is on charge will normally endeavour to effect either a repair or the movement of the casualty to some safer or more convenient place. When the damage caused to the casualty is such as to necessitate special skill or equipment, or when its location is such that it cannot be moved without the aid of a recovery vehicle, a R.E.M.E. Recovery Unit must be advised through the normal channels and in the shortest possible time, so that very early steps can be taken to recover the casualty and transport it to workshops for repair.

Any item of equipment rendered a casualty can be classified as either " X ", " Y ", " Z " or " N.R.".

"*X*" *casualties* are those in which a temporary stoppage only has occurred, or in which the damage is such that it can be repaired or rectified by the crew of the vehicle or equipment, without R.E.M.E. assistance. Typical examples of such damage are: a punctured tyre on a wheeled vehicle of a broken track pin on a tank.

"*Y*" *casualties* are those which necessitate repair by skilled personnel, but are likely to be repairable by Unit fitters or R.E.M.E. First or Second Line Workshops, provided that the general situation at the time of reporting the casualty does not alter. A simple " Y " casualty is one that can be repaired by the L.A.D. or by one of the Forward Repair Elements.

"*Z*" *casualties* are those which are beyond the capacity of the L.A.D. or Brigade Workshops, because they either require more repairs than can be carried out there, or the necessary repairs cannot be carried out on account of difficulty in reaching the casualty, lack of time, or other causes.

"*N.R.*" *casualties* (i.e., " NON-REPAIRABLE "), are those selected by Os.C. Workshops for reclamation and not for repair, hence they do not come within the scope of normal recovery operations.

" Y " AND " Z " CASUALTIES ARE THOSE WITH WHICH
R.E.M.E. RECOVERY UNITS ARE CONCERNED.

Recovery crews working under operational conditions seldom (if ever) lack work, consequently Units will normally make efforts to help themselves before enlisting the aid of a R.E.M.E. Recovery Unit. When the latter has, however, been called upon, attempts by a local Unit to recover the casualty should cease, since it must be clear to all concerned that the work to be done is outside the limitations of the equipment and experience possessed by such a Unit.

R.E.M.E.—General—G.070 refers in detail to this subject.

The Recovery System

Forward of rail or road-head, the sequence of responsibility for recovery is as follows:

(a) L.A.D.s recover from Units.

(b) Brigade Workshops recover from Units (when the recovery cannot be handled by L.A.Ds.), and from L.A.Ds or Recovery Posts to Workshop Sites or Transfer Points.

(c) Heavy and Light Sections of the Recovery Company recover and/or backload casualties to Army Collecting or Transfer points or to the appropriate third line workshops.

(d) The L. of C. Recovery Company is responsible for evacuation from the rear of Army areas to rail or road-head.

Recovery Posts

Recovery Posts—under divisional or brigade control—are established in forward areas; from these posts the Advanced Detachments of Brigade Workshops operate. A Recovery Post will be manned either by an L.A.D. or by an Advanced Workshop Detachment of a Brigade Workshop, or both.

A normal composition for the Advanced Workshop Detachments of a Brigade Workshop will probably include 2 Tractors, 6 × 4, Heavy Breakdown: 1 Lorry, 6 × 4, Breakdown and 2 Trailers, 7½ ton, 6-wheeled, Light Recovery. If necessary, a Transporter, 40-ton, Tank Recovery, can be supplied in addition, from Brigade Workshops resources. The Detachment embodies the crews of these and other vehicles, repair personnel, etc., and its size will vary according to the anticipated task.

Casualty Reporting

Three methods are normally available for this, i.e.: verbal reports, wireless reports, or Vehicle or Equipment Breakdown Cards (A.F.W. 4018). The *most rapid means available* will be employed to transmit the required information to the nearest Unit Headquarters, at which point a decision is taken to arrange *either* for the repair of the casualty *or* the handing over of the data to the nearest R.E.M.E. Unit.

Speed is essential in reporting a casualty, in order to reduce to a minimum the time lost between the occurrence of the casualty and the commencement of recovery. The potential delays prior to recovery can be summarized briefly as follows:

(a) Time taken to find the casualty and make out the Report.

(b) Time taken for the Report to reach a Unit able to take action on it.

(c) Time taken for recovery equipment to reach the casualty.

Radio contact between the Unit requesting action for recovery of a casualty, and a R.E.M.E. Recovery Unit, has many advantages. It must, however, be remembered that even though the message is in code, extreme caution is necessary to avoid betrayal to the enemy of the presence of a Unit. Moreover, a wireless silence may have to be strictly observed, in which circumstances use cannot be made of these facilities for reporting a casualty. Finally, the constant movement of Recovery Units in active zones may place them beyond wireless range.

Vehicle or Equipment Breakdown Card (A.F.W. 4018)

Prior to a recovery crew being detailed for an operation, the crew commander will have received from the officer or N.C.O. in charge of the Unit requiring R.E.M.E. assistance, the appropriate information on a Breakdown Card—see Fig. 1. This card provides on the front—see item (A) of Fig. 1—for the inclusion of such details as will enable the recovery crew commander to locate the casualty (by means of a map reference), and also gives him an accurate and comprehensive description of the casualty in respect of its type, position, damage inflicted, and replacement parts required to effect local repair (if possible). These details will assist the crew commander in his assessment of the personnel, type of vehicle, equipment, etc., required

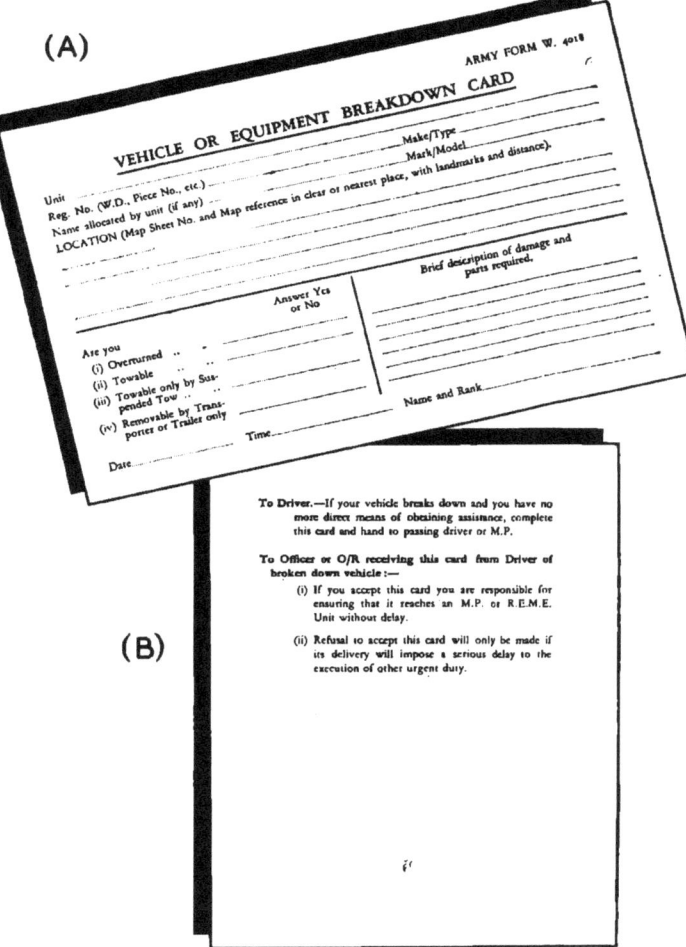

Fig. 1

for the rapid and efficient completion of the task. On the back of the card—see item (B) of Fig. 1—will be found full instructions both to the driver of the casualty vehicle and to any Officer or O.R. who may receive the card from him.

Upon the accuracy of the information given on the card will depend the initial success of the recovery operation. If the crew commander is misinformed as to the extent of the damage, he may arrive at the scene of the casualty with incorrect or insufficient equipment; if the map reference is quoted inaccurately, time will be wasted in searching for the casualty—indeed, it is by no means impossible for the crew to fall into the hands of the enemy as the direct result of such an error. The crew commander must therefore exercise great care in his interpretation of the information given, and he will be wise also to make his crew familiar with the details of the operation to be carried out—this is doubly important in case the crew commander himself should become a casualty, and be unable to continue to direct operations. In these circumstances, another member of the crew must be capable of assuming command and proceeding with the work.

Recovery Procedure

Unit Technical Officers will listen for casualty reports on the command net; they will reconnoitre and arrange assistance for those requiring it and will report to the L.A.D. casualties for which they cannot arrange repair; the L.A.D. will either:

(a) Recover and repair the casualty.

(b) Recover the casualty to a Recovery Post.

(c) If equipped with a wireless set, report to the Advanced Workshop Detachment of the Brigade Workshop that recovery is beyond L.A.D. capacity or, if a wireless set is not available, report to unit H.Q. who will transmit the report to the Brigade Workshop.

(d) Arrange for the repair of the casualty *in situ*.

(e) Recover the casualty so that the necessary repairs can be carried out at the location of the Advanced Workshop Detachment.

(f) Recover the casualty to the Brigade Workshop or to a Recovery Area and inform C.R.E.M.E. that the casualty requires repair in a third line workshop.

If a casualty requires repair in either the main body of the Brigade Workshop or in a third line workshop, it may have to be moved by transporter.

When the repair is to be carried out in the main body of the Brigade Workshops, a R.E.M.E. recovery tractor or transporter will collect the casualty, but when repair in a third line workshop is needed the casualty will be backloaded to those workshops *either* by the second line workshop concerned, *or* by the Heavy or Light Section of the Recovery Company.

In the case of tanks, backloading will be effected by R.A.S.C. Transporter Company *or* by a Heavy Recovery Section, R.E.M.E., if one is operating with the formation.

Wheeled transporters will only be allowed to move forward and collect casualties *when roads are available*, and in accordance with the divisional recovery plan.

Routing and Initial Reconnaissance

Before proceeding to the casualty, the crew commander must be satisfied that the route selected is suitable for both outward and homeward journeys. Bridge classifications and heights, width and surface conditions of roads, etc., are important features to be considered, and must be checked on the outward journey if it is intended to return over the same route. Personnel, must remain vigilant and alert for signs of enemy patrols, and, if the possibility of contact with the enemy exists, evasive action and passive defence measures must be adopted to safeguard both recovery equipment and crew.

The shortest route to the location may not prove in the long run to be the most suitable. Consider carefully when routing; always avoid danger, since risks taken unnecessarily may involve the loss of the crew, the recovery vehicle(s) and the equipment.

Pack rations should be provided for each member of the crew, and when the recovery operation is likely to occupy a considerable length of time, additional emergency rations must be carried. The cooker, Portable, No. 2, carried on each recovery vehicle, is provided for the preparation of such meals as time and circumstances permit. For further details of the cooker, see Section "Appliances," Part III.

When necessary (and if available), a motor cyclist will be attached to the recovery crew to act as vanguard and guide. Common-sense considerations will decide whether or not it is necessary to use the motor cyclist: for example, in friendly territory where the route is familiar and risks are negligible, he might serve no particular purpose. On the other hand, even in friendly territory where the route is unfamiliar, the motor cyclist will prove an asset both in warning the driver of a recovery vehicle of dangerous points ahead, and in taking over traffic control at road crossings, etc.

The Final Reconnaissance

In battle areas the motor cyclist is of very great value to the recovery crew, since he will not only act as a guide but also warn the crew of the enemy's presence. In this connection, he must observe great caution, since the noise of the motor cycle engine will be likely to betray his presence to the enemy. Upon nearing the scene of the casualty, the motor cyclist will halt at an assembly point predetermined by the crew commander and await the arrival of the recovery detail which is following. On assembly, the crew commander will, if in hostile territory, face a number of alternatives, and one of those detailed below should be adopted:

1. The crew commander may order the crew and motor cyclist (on foot to extend and carry out a reconnaissance covering the approaches and area surrounding the casualty, the driver remaining with the recovery vehicle.

2. The crew commander himself may proceed on foot (or use the motor cycle), and carry out an individual reconnaissance—the crew and motor cyclist remaining with the vehicle.

2. The crew commander may detail the motor cyclist to reconnoitre the approaches and scene of the casualty.

In friendly territory, however, the approach to the casualty will not warrant such precautions.

The driver, meanwhile, will park the recovery vehicle under cover, or effect camouflage with the appropriate equipment and such natural aids as may be available—in no circumstances must he leave the vehicle.

The importance of the reconnaissance cannot be over-emphasised; the ground *en route* and in the vicinity of the casualty may be mined; booby traps may (and probably will) also be encountered; the casualty itself may even be occupied by enemy troops. DO NOT, THEREFORE, UNDER-RATE THE DANGERS INVOLVED IN RECOVERY OPERATIONS —THE ENEMY WILL DO ALL HE CAN TO MAKE THEM DIFFICULT. Remember—*always* approach the casualty cautiously; send only one man out first, and that in the direction of the casualty's blind spot—it may be that your fears will prove unfounded but it is not worth while taking a chance.

In the event of the locality or scene of the casualty being occupied by the enemy, the scout will immediately return and with the remainder of the recovery crew assembled, the crew commander will give the order to withdraw.

Should the crew commander reassure himself that it is safe to proceed with the recovery operation, he will post a sentry to patrol between points which command a full view of the operation and its surroundings. The motor cyclist should fill the role of sentry, and since he is not a member of the actual recovery crew, the effective working strength of the latter will thus remain unimpaired.

In daylight, the sentry will adopt the normal signals used in the field to indicate an approach by the enemy—all personnel having been made acquainted with these signals during their training. At night, the approach of the enemy will necessitate audible warning, care being taken to pre-determine the signals and ensure that they are well known to the whole crew.

Side arms and equipment of recovery personnel will not be worn during the actual recovery, but must be placed within easy reach so that each man can rapidly arm himself in the event of enemy intervention.

TERRAIN

Section 1.—INFLUENCE OF TERRAIN ON RECOVERY WORK

(a) Nature of Terrain

Recovery personnel must have a good general knowledge of the nature of the various kinds of terrain likely to be met with in military operations, not only on account of the widely differing surfaces, but also because of the variations in the *soil bearing characteristics*—in other words, the ability of the ground to withstand the loads likely to be imposed on it through the use of wheeled and tracked vehicles, jacks, skidding, holdfast spikes and other forms of earth anchor, etc.

It is only to a very limited extent that recovery crews can predetermine the nature of the terrain on which their work is to be carried out, and then only by extricating a casualty vehicle from its original position (possibly from the surrounding ground as well), and towing it to a more convenient, harder patch where repairs can be effected, the casualty made mobile or, alternatively, loaded on to a transporter.

The principal problem facing recovery personnel in connection with terrain is, therefore, the correct understanding of the various natures of soils (including surface and subsoils) and their bearing capacities, so that wherever the casualty may lie its recovery can, within certain limits, be effected with speed and safety.

Most of the terrain experienced will fall into one or other of the categories discussed in the appropriate paragraphs, but it should be appreciated that there may be a considerable mixture of types in any given area, due to the geological formation of the ground. In order to make this clear, refer to

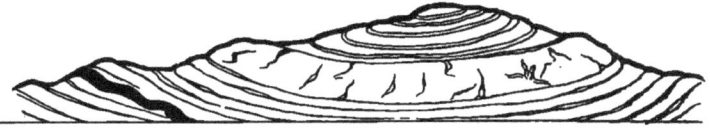

Fig. 2

Fig. 2, which shows one of the many ways in which the strata of the ground may have been caused to vary from point to point, as the result of natural disturbances of the underlying rocks.

(b) Altitude of terrain

Quite apart from the nature of the actual terrain itself, altitude has a profound influence on recovery operations. There is, first of all, an increase at high altitude in the fatigue induced in personnel as the result of their activities—the reduction in oxygen content of the atmosphere is the direct cause of this phenomenon. Moreover, increases in altitude cause a marked falling-off in the power output of internal combustion engines, hence the maximum drawbar pull of any particular vehicle will be correspondingly reduced—although the weights and resistances of casualties will, of course, be the same as at lower levels.

The physical effects of high altitudes on personnel should be clearly understood. If one rises suddenly above sea level, the tissues suffer from "oxygen want", which is more pronounced during excercise and shows itself by the individual becoming breathless. The body compensates for this by increasing the number of red blood corpuscles and thus more oxygen can reach the tissues. This increase in red blood corpuscles requires from a number of hours up to two or three days to take place, according to the height reached.

There is, in addition to the increase in red blood corpuscles, a process of acclimatisation to be accomplished. This varies in different subjects and at different ranges of altitude; for example, at altitudes from 6,000 ft. to 10,000 ft. acclimatisation would normally take about 2 weeks, whereas at altitudes in the neighbourhood of 14,000 ft. the process would take between 2 and 3 weeks. Even when the process is complete, however, the maximum exercise tolerance is reduced at high altitude.

Conservation of energy is extremely important in mountainous country, and must be practised on every occasion, noting particularly the following points:

(a) Travel light — Everything that is not absolutely necessary must be left behind. At the end of a long day every ounce counts.

(b) Route ... Importance of good route choosing cannot be over-estimated.

(c) Rhythm ... Walk up-hill at an easy swing and try to attain rhythm. DO NOT go up-hill in a rapid spurt with frequent halts; an easy pace will carry you further and find you fresher at the end.

(d) Balance ... Is essential in rough mountainous country; never over step yourself by taking one step where two could more easily have been taken.

Due allowance must be made for these features in all recovery estimates and calculations based on high altitude operations.

Section 2.—PRACTICAL DETAILS OF VEHICULAR MOVEMENT

The natural conditions which result in failure on the part of a vehicle or other military equipment to cross a certain piece of ground and thus to become a casualty on (or in) it, will largely affect the performance of any vehicle sent out to effect recovery. It is therefore essential that full weight shall be given to such data as is available regarding the manner in which both wheeled and tracked vehicles are caused to move. Much experimental and development work has yet to be carried out on this important problem, but certain facts have already been established.

(a) **Causes of failure to move**

There are two primary causes of failure to move on the part of a vehicle:

(i) Excessive sinkage.
(ii) Excessive slip.

Dealing first with the question of sinkage, this is a function of the weight of the vehicle in relation to the area which is in contact with the ground—in other words, the weight resting on each square inch of the track or tyre which is effective in supporting the vehicle. If a vehicle is left standing for an appreciable period on soft ground it will sink under its own weight—this is primarily due to the fact that the ground is squeezed out from under the tracks or tyres and flows outwards, thus allowing the vehicle to sink into the space left vacant.

Speed has a very considerable influence on sinkage—particularly in the case of heavy vehicles. A golden rule in recovery work is— "keep moving as long as possible". The *combined* effect on soil of *pressure* and *shear* reduces its supporting power to a marked extent—this explains why a vehicle in motion may be able to keep going on *flat* ground, whereas even a slight incline would cause a stoppage to occur. As soon as a heavy vehicle stops in soft ground it commences to sink and thereby increases the effort needed to recommence movement later on.

In connection with the problem of excessive slip, it must be observed that in the majority of cases the primary cause of the failure of the vehicle to " keep moving " is the low shear strength of the ground immediately under the tracks or wheels.

This is well exemplified by the Chains, Overall, which are applied to the rear driving wheels of certain 6 × 4 vehicles. The rubber tyres of these vehicles—whilst provided with carefully designed treads adapted to engage with rough terrain—soon shear off portions of the surface soil when the going is very soft, thereby filling up all the grooves in the tread. By fitting Chains, Overall (see "Appliances" Section, Part I), the area of ground exposed to shear is multiplied many times over and the wheels thereby enabled to regain a firm grip. Similar remarks apply in the case of the " Grousers " fitted to the tracks of certain Armoured Recovery Vehicles.

A further consideration arises in connection with excessive slip—the "milling cutter" action which occurs due to the grooved tracks or tyres churning in the surface of the soil. If this is continued to its logical conclusion, the vehicle will gradually settle down in the ground until the belly (in the case of a tank) or the front axle, crankcase and rear axle (in the case of a wheeled vehicle and according to the disposition of the driving wheels), has reached the point of pressure balance for that particular type of soil.

Driving considerations enter very much into the effect of terrain on vehicle movements. Good driving will frequently extricate a bogged vehicle—or enable it to continue on its way—whilst bad driving will cause still further bogging down to occur. This aspect of the handling of recovery vehicles is dealt with in the appropriate section of " Technique, Part II—Practical Aspects of Recovery".

(b) **Colour of soil as an index to "trafficability"**

Colour of soil or of vegetation	Normal index to trafficability
ALL LIGHT-COLOURED SOILS	Indicate water percolating soils that may be either chalky, gravelly, or sandy. They usually provide good going. The one exception is the sticky or sandy yellow clay generally to be found locally in chalk and limestone country.
BROWN SOILS	The depth of hue of brown soils varies much with the degree of dampness (darkening with dampness). Generally, brown soils provide good going except in undrained depressions which may touch the level of the water table; but brown soils that are a very deep brown when dry tend to be heavy and sticky when very wet.
RED SOILS ...	There are two kinds of red soil: (i) That which is derived from limestones and has a rich, bright, brown-russet hue. This is a light soil which normally affords good going. (ii) That which is a clay and has a duller hue of maroon or even purple-red. This soil makes heavy going when wet and may be very bad.
GREY SLATE-COLOURED SOILS	Indicates heavy clay.
BLACK SOIL	Indicates peat, often soft and wet—very bad going and often impassable for tanks.

(c) **Effect of the moisture content of the soil**

There is ample evidence to show that soil conditions vary considerably from day to day—in some cases, from hour to hour—and that this variation is sufficient to affect vehicular movement across such ground.

Moisture has, of course, a pronounced influence on this, but the nature of the soil itself is also of the greatest importance—see later paragraphs dealing with "Clay" and "Loam".

After a piece of ground has become impassable to vehicles as the result of natural conditions or churning up due to the passage of tracks or wheels, it may be necessary merely to wait for the moisture to drain away or for the wind to dry the surface, when the soil will again become usable to vehicles of one class or another. These remarks are particularly applicable to "brick-earth" areas.

(d) **Effect of vegetation**

The effect of vegetation on the performance of vehicles depends on the type of vegetation, but as a general rule tracked vehicles fitted with spudded tracks grip the roots of small shrubs or grass—whether wet or dry—and give an additional resistance to slip.

With a wheeled vehicle, if the vegetation is at all wet it reduces the gripping power of rubber tyres, but otherwise is an improvement.

It can be concluded, therefore, that where the vegetation has been worn away by traffic there will be a higher rate of deterioration due to moisture than on virgin soil and a reduction in performance of both wheeled and tracked vehicles will result when wet.

Section 3.—SOIL MECHANICS

Soil mechanics is the study of the characteristics and physical properties of soils.

Whilst considerable research has been carried out in the past on engineering earth formations such as structural foundations, dams, etc., there has, until quite recently, been comparatively little information available as to the behaviour of surface and sub-soils when subjected to the rolling action of wheels or tracks—particularly during conditions of extreme wetness or dryness.

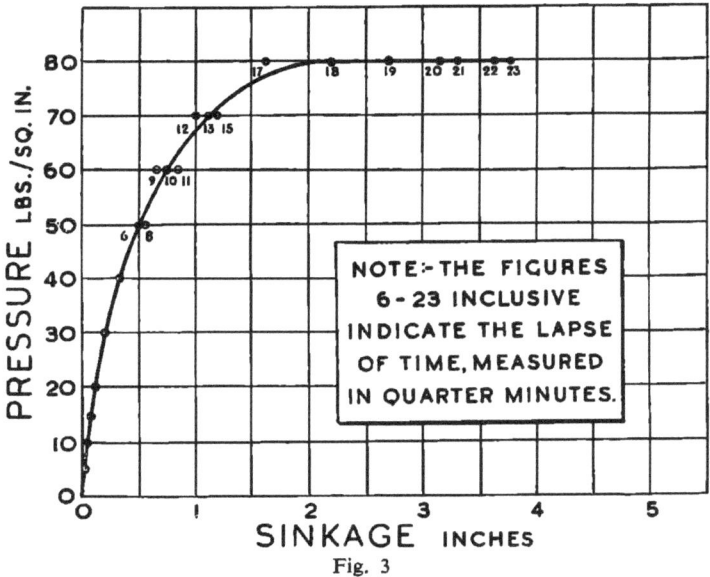

Fig. 3

Soils vary widely, both in chemical composition, the size and shape of the particles of which they are composed and the amount of moisture contained, In any soil, when pressure is applied sinkage occurs; this increases gradually with the pressure until what is called the " yield point " is reached, after which failure occurs and additional sinkage takes place with little or no additional load. A typical example of this is shown in Fig. 3, which gives the result of a trial carried out on a wet, clay-loam soil during the winter time; from this the yield point is found to be 80 lbs./sq. in.

The pressure which a soil will resist before failure occurs is known as its *bearing Capacity* and failure is due to *Shear*, at which point all cohesion between the particles ceases. For further data concerning these terms (in relation to the general subject of Strength of Materials), see the appropriate section—" Technique, Part II—Technical Aspects of Recovery".

Various formulæ have been evolved to give the bearing capacity of a soil, and from the results of these the following table of bearing capacities has been prepared.

The term " cohesion " (measured in lbs./sq. in.), represents the tendency of the soil particles to stick together even when there is no normal pressure, and is therefore taken to be a constant which is *independent of normal pressure*.

TABLE OF SOIL BEARING CAPACITIES
ON STRIPS OF VARYING WIDTH

Type of Soil	Cohesion (lbs./sq. in)	Bearing Capacities (lbs./sq. in.)	
		On strip 6" wide	On strip 60" wide
Silts (wet)	0	0.1	1.0
Sands (dry)	0	1.9	18.8
Sands (immersed)	0	1.2	11.9
Clay (liquid)	0.7	2.8	2.8
„ (very soft)	1.4	6.0	6.1
„ (soft)	2.8	12.9	13.1
„ (fairly stiff)	13.9	34.6	35.0
„ (very stiff)	27.8	86.7	88.0
" Cemented " sand and gravel (wet)	3.5	61.2	78.0
" Cemented " sand and gravel (dry)	6.9	129.0	137.2

It is particularly interesting to note that *when cohesion is zero the width of the strip affects the results very greatly* and that as cohesion increases the width is of decreasing importance. This is a phenomenon well known in recovery work, since the greater the area on which a load is applied (as in the case of a number of gun planks laid side by side: or the wide, flat tracks of the Transporter, Tracked, 45-ton, Tank Recovery), the less does the ground tend to squeeze (or " spew ") out from the sides of the surface under load. In other words, the grounds tends to become *trapped* under the flat surface, in a manner somewhat similar to mud-boards which, when strapped to the feet, enable a person to traverse extremely soft surfaces.

Consider a wheel as at (A), Fig. 4, which has sunk in the ground until the resistance of the soil is equal to the weight on the wheel, and then suppose the wheel to move forward to the right until it is in position (B), Fig. 4. The ground under the lowest point of the wheel is depressed deepest and the sinkage gradually decreases round the wheel to the point where contact between wheel and ground ceases; as the wheel advances, therefore, a channel or rut is formed whose depth is approximately that of the lowest point reached by the wheel.

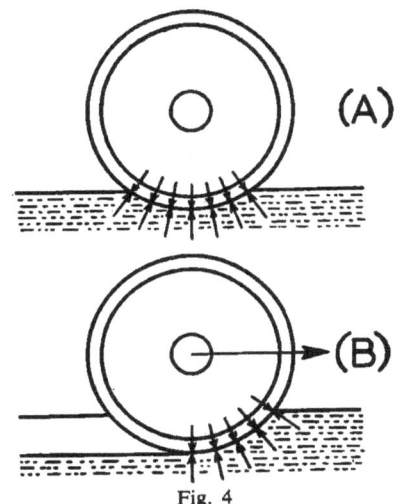

Fig. 4

It will be noticed that the wheel at (B) has penetrated the ground more deeply than the one shown at (A), because it is only the earth beneath the arc to the right of the wheel at (B) which is supporting the weight of the advancing wheel—i.e., roughly *half the area shown at* (A).

If it is now supposed that an articulating or flexible tank track—any one of those commonly employed—surrounds the wheel, and that this extends backwards along the ground in the usual manner, it is evident that theoretically the track *between* the wheels can exert no pressure on the ground nor can it support any weight owing to its flexibility. Such a " band " stretched between two points can only withstand pressure if it is *curved*. Form this it follows that the weight of a tracked vehicle is by no means evenly distributed over the total area of its tracks, and that in actual fact the track will sink very much more deeply than might be pre-supposed.

The *tension* in the track plays a very important part in the operation of a tracked vehicle, since the greater the tension the more nearly will the track act as a girder and take its full share of the weight. (For details of a track which is constructed on a " rigid girder " principle, see Section " Recovery Vehicles by Types—Transporter, Tracked, 45-ton, Tank Recovery). The possible tension in a flexible type track is, however, limited by considerations other than specific ground pressure, consequently the recommended tension must never be exceeded purely in order to accomplish more uniform load distribution on the tracks.

Tank tracks and suspensions vary widely in details and in some the vehicle weight is distributed over the tracks more evenly than in others. It is, however, safe to assume that a maximum of only 30% of the total track area supports the weight of the vehicle (except in the case of the Churchill tank), hence anticipated sinkages should be based on this figure and *not* on the ground pressure obtained as the result of dividing the total weight of the vehicle by the area of the tracks in contact with the ground.

To see how this works out in actual practice, take as an example a 20-ton tank with tracks 12" wide and 10' 6" long in contact with the ground (i.e., 3,000 sq. ins. approx.). The mean pressure would appear to be only 15 lbs. per sq. in. but if we take only 30% of the area (or 900 sq. ins.), the mean pressure will be raised to about 50 *lbs. per sq. in.;* in practice it will be found that the sinkage will roughly correspond to such a figure. The Churchill tank, however, which has a relatively large number of small diameter wheels, presents a special case. Here, the maximum of 30% of the total track area will be exceeded, but for recovery purposes this increase may normally be neglected since its effect is but to simplify or ease the recovery problem to some extent.

Unless a track is rolling on a smooth hard surface—which is seldom the case—a substantial amount of power is consumed in depressing the ground under the tracks. This is largely wasted energy, and is of vital importance in recovery work since it is a measure of the pull needed to tow the vehicle from a position in which it has become a casualty. The pull needed to move a rolling casualty on level ground is a function of the ground resistance, wheel diameter and the width of tyre or track. All these conditions must be borne in mind when estimating.

Whilst much technical investigation work remains to be done on this subject of rolling resistance, practical considerations demand a guide to the *approximate* values which must be allotted to casualty vehicles of one sort or another when lying on (or in) various kinds of terrain.

A number of measurements have been made covering rolling resistances on hard ground, either by measuring directly the pull required or by cutting off the power and plotting the distance then covered by the vehicle, but so far little data is available as to why one type of track offers more resistance than another, or more resistance on one day than another. It is, however, reasonable to assume that the average rolling resistance of a tracked vehicle *on hard ground* is about 4 lbs. per 100 lbs. of vehicle weight and in the example quoted above (a 20-ton tank), the rolling resistance would be 16 cwts.—i.e., $\dfrac{\text{Weight of vehicle.}}{25}$

When soft ground is encountered, however, conditions are quite different because much energy is required to consolidate the soil until it can support the weight of the vehicle.

The following approximate figures (based entirely upon experimental results), can be used for normal rolling casualties:

Smooth road	$\dfrac{\text{Weight of Vehicle}}{25}$	Sand: hard, wet	$\dfrac{\text{Weight of Vehicle}}{6}$
Grass	$\dfrac{\text{Weight of Vehicle}}{7}$	,, soft, wet	$\dfrac{\text{Weight of Vehicle}}{5}$
Gravel	$\dfrac{\text{Weight of Vehicle}}{5}$	,, loose, dry	$\dfrac{\text{Weight of Vehicle}}{4}$
Shingle Beach	$\dfrac{\text{Weight of Vehicle}}{3}$	Black mud ...	$\dfrac{\text{Weight of Vehicle}}{2}$
	Soft blue clay ... $\dfrac{\text{Weight of vehicle}}{2}$		

Section 4—TYPES OF TERRAIN

(a) **Surface Soils**

The term "surface soil" is normally applied to that portion of the ground which is capable of being cultivated—i.e. that which lies between (say) 2" to 4" deep in the more barren areas, and up to about 10" deep in the well-cultivated areas. Good plough-land, for example, will normally have a surface soil depth of around 7" to 9", with a readily permeable subsoil, whilst a hillside (grass-covered) will frequently have no more than 3" of soil covering a subsoil of rock or stones of a highly impermeable nature.

There are two main types of surface soils—*(a)* the natural or virgin (i.e. that which has not been cultivated), and *(b)* the more or less artificial or cultivated soil, which is a modified condition of the natural soil and is therefore liable to be soft, due to constant working and the addition of humus of one sort or another.

Virgin soil may be hard or soft, according to its location—for example, in peaty or marshy country the ground will clearly be very soft and treacherous, whilst on exposed hillsides—the surface soil depth of which is often less than 4" on a rocky subsoil—the ground will normally be firm (but see following data relating to bogs and rocky outcrops).

Cultivated soils vary within the widest possible limits insofar as the passage of vehicles is concerned. At one end of the scale are the light sandy soils—varying in colour from jet black through grey, fawn, and yellow to a deep red—whilst at the other end of the scale are the heavier, sticky soils such as clayey-loam, brick-earth, loess, adobe, etc.

Desert sand must be regarded as both surface soil and subsoil, since its depth is a variable, dependent on the location of the underlying hard strata, and the effects of prevailing winds. Normally, however, desert sand is interspersed with rocky outcrops and hard areas, with occasional salt marshes.

(b) **Subsoils**

Casualty vehicles are seldom so light in weight that they will rest on top of the surface soil, and it is, therefore, with the nature of the underlying portions of the surface soil and the various subsoils that recovery personnel are frequently concerned—particularly the ability to withstand compressive and shear stresses.

The general formation of the top surface of the earth's crust is shown in Fig. 5, in which the surface soil is shown at (A—A), the subsoil at (B—B), and the lower rocky strata from which the subsoil is formed at (C—C). The general process of soil formation causes a gradual transference from (C) to (A) by weathering, effects of water, frost and snow, working of the soil by agriculture, etc.

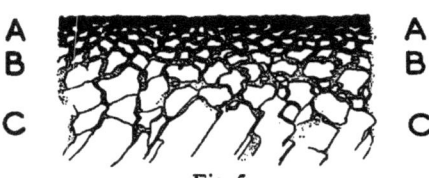

Fig 5

The principal forms of subsoil likely to be met with in recovery are as follows:

CLAY.—This may occur in its pure form (as in the white china-clays), or may contain fine sand or silt, chalky or carbonaceous matter (as in the various yellowish, red or brown clays). When in close proximity to a river

Fig. 6

mouth, where a large amount of alluvial matter may be present, clay deposits are likely to be of the bluish-grey variety (see Fig. 6).

Fig. 7

From a recovery point of view, clay often presents problems. If thoroughly wet (as shown in Fig. 7), it is likely to prove very resistant to motion—wheel spin inside the overall chains was induced at the rear wheels of the driving bogie of this transporter. On the other hand, if only partially wetted, clay becomes " greasy " and difficulties once more arise in connection with the tractive effort of recovery vehicles and the suction effect produced on, say, a bellied tank.

Holdfast located in clay soil will normally prove satisfactory, but the pins are often difficult to remove owing to the suction effect above referred to.

Great care must be taken when proceeding with vehicles over clay ground which has been broken up by transport, shell-fire or bombing, especially when the surface has subsequently been dried out by the wind. In such a case, the top surface is likely to give way suddenly and cause the wheels or tracks of both casualty and recovery vehicles to sink without warning, thus producing further problems.

SHALE.—A clayey rock, thinly bedded or laminated, which splits into layers along the plane of its bedding; it frequently weathers into clay.

Normally, shale may be expected to stand a heavier load than clay, in view of its laminated form—particularly in those cases where there is a tendency for the shale to become transformed into sandstone. Holdfast spikes will usually penetrate shale without difficulty, and will give a good hold.

MARL.—This is a natural mixture of clay and *chalk*—the latter being very finely divided. Marl is markedly lighter in weight than clay, and is much more friable—i.e. it breaks up into fine powder on being exposed to the air. Normally, marl is likely to present problems in recovery (particularly when wet), and its ability to withstand compressive and shear stresses is comparatively low.

LOAM.—This term should not be confused with that frequently employed to describe a surface soil of particularly high fertility. The correct definition of loam is a natural mixture of clay and *sand*, particularly valuable as " brick-earth ". This application gives a clue to its properties in connection with recovery; loam is not as " sticky " as clay (even when wetted), and is therefore less liable to offer resistance to the passage of a casualty vehicle. In general, loam will carry a fairly heavy weight without undue sinkage, will stand the strain of a holdfast, and (due to its brick-forming propensities), will harden in the air so as normally to permit the safe passage of a vehicle.

LOESS.—Loess is a chalky loam of porous structure, buff in colour and occurring in accumulations of great superficial area and depth—particularly on the continent of Europe. It contains land (and occasionally freshwater) shells, the local composition consequently varying though general uniformity in character is maintained. Loess is crumbly when handled, though in bulk it is homogeneous, and sufficiently tenacious to stand in precipitous or even vertical cliffs up to 200 feet high along the borders of valleys.

ADOBE.—This is a clay of somewhat similar nature to loess, and is a silt mixed with coarser chalky matter. It is chiefly found in countries in which occur streams normally having a rapid rate of flow, but which periodically slacken speed and so carry off only the clay and a few heavier particles to other places. Adobe is grey-brown or yellow in colour, porous and friable, and when wetted and allowed to dry sets with a hardness approaching that of concrete. Recovery problems in areas containing adobe are likely to be confined to the securing of a satisfactory holdfast in the damper areas. In dry areas, the hard nature of the dried clay renders it an ideal material over which to recover.

SILT.—The fine-grained muddy sand or sedimentary deposit washed down by a river into its estuary is called silt, and as such falls within the category of " hinterland "—viz. the area which lies between a sea beach and the land beyond—see Fig. 8, which shows such a typical area. It

Fig. 8

should be noted, however, that hinterland will often include dry areas such as that shown in Fig. 16. Silt is usually highly compressible, though any increase in the sand content tends to stabilize it.

From a recovery standpoint, silt represents an extremely difficult (and sometimes dangerous) kind of terrain—particularly when water is likely to rise (or flow) through it, since in such circumstances it loses all its stability. Firstly, it is practically impossible to obtain a secure hold with any form of steel holdfast spike (baulk holdfasts only may be relied upon); secondly, a casualty located on silt is likely to be bellied and therefore to represent a major recovery problem; and thirdly, the approach to the casualty by a recovery vehicle is likely to be hazardous owing to sinkage. This, then, is clearly a case for a long tow rope, with the recovery vehicle off the area of the silt.

SAND.—Land sand (as distinct from sea sand) is very widely distributed. When met with as a subsoil, it is normally in a damp and comparatively solid state, and hence will withstand a fairly high compressive stress. Its ability to withstand shear, however, is severely limited, and the maintenance of a holdfast in a sandy subsoil is frequently a matter of some difficulty.

When dry, grains of sand provide no hold whatsoever for the wheels or tracks of vehicles, unless their area of contact is extremely large. For this reason, pneumatic-tyred vehicles have their tyre pressures lowered when travelling across sand, so as to increase the area in contact with the ground—see D.M.E. Technical Instruction No. B.400 and subsequent amendments.

Fig. 9

Tracked vehicles also, operate with greater facility on sand when their specific track pressure is low. Desert sand—which is often of an extremely fine and dusty character—constitutes a " surface soil " as well as a subsoil.

Fig 9 shows the kind of terrain commonly met with in the desert (Libya)—soft wind-blown sand with coarse grass and, in some places, scrub. In general, desert terrain includes one or more of the following :

    (a) Patches of loose wind-blown sand; these are normally found under the lee of a hill.

    (b) Crusted desert, i.e. a crust of pebbly ground with soft sand underneath.

    (c) Boulders.

    (d) Small hillocks of sand formed round bushes.

    (e) Wadis or nullahs, often with steep sides and soft sandy beds.

    (f) Hump-backed irrigation channels.

    (g) Railway crossings. A railway line often forms a confusing obstacle especially when carried on low embankments.

Fig. 10

GRAVEL.—This is a mixture of hard stones (pebbles or angular fragments), with sand of a siliceous (and often ferruginous) character. In some gravels the sand is distinctly " clayey ", and hence greater ability to " pack " is experienced. Normally, gravel presents no difficulty from the standpoint of its bearing capacity, owing to its ability to discharge any surface water, but it does frequently present a problem when laying a holdfast—the spikes have a tendency to foul the pebbles or stones and are thus troublesome to insert.

ROCKS.—Scattered or " tumbled " rocks such as limestone boulders are often to be found on hillsides, as shown in Fig. 10 (a view of a part of Tunisia over which fighting has taken place), and they may form a serious obstacle if present in large numbers.

Owing to the general proximity of rock to the surface of the soil in mountainous, hilly or moorland districts, it is difficult to find a hold for the spikes of earth anchors, as the underlying material is much too hard for these to penetrate. Where a rocky outcrop is of such a form as to *appear* to offer a convenient natural holdfast, it should be used with caution, as it may give way when a load is applied. Experience, judgment or careful testing must decide whether or not the rock will stand up to the load

Fig. 11

which it is proposed to apply, and where there is the slightest doubt, it should *not* be used.

Occasionally, large half-hidden rocks of the type seen in Fig. 11 are encountered in mountainous districts and high moorlands. The smooth surface of such rocks is due to ice action during the glacial period when the normally irregular formation of the rock was gradually worn away. The terrain where they occur is but thinly covered with soil and, particularly

Fig. 12

in the neighbourhood of the outcrop, the layer may easily be cut away by vehicle tracks, leaving a surface upon which neither wheels nor tracks are able to obtain a sure grip.

Fig. 12—a scene from the Italian campaign—shows a mountain area of the type in which recovery operations may have to be carried out.

(c) Marshes, Bogs, Swamps and Jungle

PEAT.—Peat, which invariably occurs in virgin soil, is formed by the growth and decay of plants in boggy or marshy areas where the water is stagnant, and is generally to be found over a bed of clay or shale; in some parts of the country the peat foundations are covered with a layer of fine white sand.

The upper portion of a peat bed is light brown and spongy, whilst lower down the peat is (much darker—almost black. It may attain, in places, a thickness of 50 feet or more. Although formed chiefly in temperate climates, peaty accumulations may arise in tropical countries by the decay of vegetation in swamps—e.g. mangrove swamps.

There are two distinct varieties of peaty terrain:
- (a) Lowland, marsh, or bog peat, formed in stagnant pools or more or less rocky basins.
- (b) Hill or mountain peat, which is formed at various elevations.

The lowland peat includes the more extensive tracts in the marshlands and valleys, whilst the hill or mountain peat is usually to be found under a top coating of heather (fibrous " turf ").

When wet, peat is troublesome to recovery crews, for it provides a much-reduced hold for tracked vehicles, and wheeled vehicles frequently develop " wheel-spin ". Attempts to produce a firm road or track over very soft peat almost invariably end in failure since the " fill " tends to sink into and be absorbed by the plastic peat. To make progress with vehicles on this terrain, it is sometimes found useful to lay down brushwood in order to consolidate the ground and provide a grip, but care must be taken to ensure that the peaty area does not run into a bog.

BOG.—It is not always fully appreciated that bogs are to be found on both high and low ground—it is a fallacy that bogs and swamps are synonymous terms. A bog usually has a clay bottom—frequently with a thick coating of white sand—but bogs also occur where vegetation has produced an *artificially* impervious subsoil, as, for example, in various depressions to be found in Southern England. Over the bog bottom (of whatever origin) is supported, by a quantity of water, the peat of which the bog is formed. The upper portions of the peat may be (or appear to be) perfectly dry, whilst the lower parts will be waterlogged, the passage of a vehicle wheel (or even a human footstep) on the top surface being sufficient to produce oscillation of the floating mass of peat.

The depth of a bog of this nature may vary from a few inches to many feet, and its greatest danger lies in the fact that it may *almost* provide the required support, but at the crucial moment the surface may break and engulf the vehicle or person attempting its passage.

Recovery from a deep bog is almost an impossibility—particularly when the vehicle is completely submerged—but in cases where the depth of penetration is only two or three feet, the attempt should be made. Recovery vehicles and holdfasts must be kept on hard ground, away from the boggy area altogether, and the greatest care must be taken to see that personnel do not expose themselves to unnecessary risks.

In certain cases bogs have been known to burst; this occurs chiefly in the case of hillside bogs, after heavy rains have fallen on a large tract of peat. When a bog bursts (usually at its lowest end), a considerable volume of peaty water will flow down into the areas below, carrying with it a quantity of surface peat.

MARSH.—Marshy or swampy ground in temperate climates is clearly distinguished from bog or peat by the presence of fresh green vegetation, and, by the well-known marsh grasses. Normally, marsh is based on the sedimentary material (clays, marls, loams, sands and silts, etc.) carried down by rivers and streams, and caused to accumulate in an area where it can remain waterlogged. Flooding may (and probably will) occur at intervals, and this will have the effect of rendering still more difficult a recovery operation conducted on such terrain.

Quite apart from the fact that holdfasts cannot be used in marshy ground the wheels or tracks of recovery vehicles are apt to sink deeply and may even result in the latter becoming casualties themselves. There is, however, not nearly so much danger of complete submersion of vehicles and personnel as in the case of a bog. Whenever practicable, tracked recovery vehicles should be used for operations in marshy areas.

TROPICAL SWAMPS.—The duration of the wet season (or " rains ") in tropical countries varies according to the latitude, lasting over a period of from two to six months. Whether of long or short duration, however, the precipitation is always high in the tropics and is usually measured in *feet* rather than in *inches*.

Such vast tonnages descending on the higher lands eventually flow—in a series of gullies of varying width and depth—to the flatter parts near the coast, carrying with them quantities of mineral and vegetable matter. As the velocity of flow decreases, the bulk of the solids carried in suspension is deposited, producing great stretches of waterlogged debris—usually in the form of a fertile swamp criss-crossed with innumerable water channels.

The heavier material brought down forms a more or less impervious base and the numerous " islands " between the water areas only dry out superficially. After the cessation of the rains, the water in these flat terrains becomes stagnant and forms a breeding ground for various insects, including the mosquito.

Fig 13.

In their natural condition such swamps are practically impassable, but by local draining and filling, tracks capable of carrying vehicles may be constructed across them.

Any recovery operation which has to be effected on (or over) such terrain is essentially difficult. Normally, no mechanical earth anchor or holdfast can be used, and the only safe method of operation is to rely upon direct haulage through the medium of a recovery tractor and tow rope (the tractor in such a case being, preferably, of the tracked variety. As an example of actual recovery in progress in a tropical swamp, see Fig. 13, which shows troops of the South West Pacific Area forces at work.

Special attention must be paid during recovery operations in tropical swamps—also when working in the jungle (see following paragraphs)—to allow for the effect of the climate on personnel engaged.

The *humidity is likely to be very high*—varying from 80% to 98%.

The *temperature in the shade may lie around* 90° F. with a *sun temperature of up to* 165° F.

The effect of these conditions on personnel is enervating, and they cannot, therefore, normally carry or sustain loads in excess of about 40 lb. each, although for very limited periods loads up to 60 lb. may be carried. This point is of especial importance when the approach to the casualty is on foot over any distance—particularly when long tow ropes, chackles, etc., have to be carried.

Fig. 14

JUNGLE.—A jungle is a tropical forest choked with undergrowth (see Fig. 14, which shows a jungle in New Guinea). The virgin soil, watered by torrential rains and usually aided by a continuously high humidity, teems with every variety of vegetation. With the passage of time the latter becomes a tangled mat of almost impenetrable density and offers one of the most serious natural obstacles to the passage of vehicles—of whatever description.

Jungle terrain is also frequently precipitous, rugged and rocky, the torrents resulting from the intense rainfall already referred to causing gullies or gorges which follow every natural depression in their descent to the lower levels.

Although military operations make it essential to force a passage through such undergrowth, this is frequently only possible by following a line of least resistance coupled with a certain amount of unavoidable clearing, the intersecting gullies being crossed without much danger if the water is not too deep or swift.

Fig. 15

In this connection see Fig. 15, which, whilst not depicting a recovery scene, may serve to show the kind of terrain under discussion and the extent to which man-handling has sometimes to be employed—particularly in connection with artillery.

Recovery problems in the jungle are likely to reside principally in:
 (i) the passage of the recovery vehicle to the scene of the casualty and
 (ii) the return journey to workshops with the casualty in tow.

An adequate supply of natural holdfasts (in the form of trees) will be found ready to hand. Many occasions will arise in which self-recovery means prove themselves useful in assisting progress through areas in which the path already cleared is insufficiently wide for the available recovery vehicle to traverse.

SALTINGS AND THE HINTERLAND OF SEA BEACHES.—A special kind of marsh is that known as a " salting "—an area so near to the sea that at certain periods of the year (if not at each tide) it either becomes covered or is well intersected by sea water through the medium of runnels. Saltings

Fig. 16

may be considerably below sea level, hence care must be employed to observe whether or not there is sufficient time to recover a casualty before the tide has risen—this is particularly necessary in the event of the casualty having been trapped in a runnel—see Fig. 8.

Normally, the ground of which saltings are composed is a rich clayey loam, with patches of peat and a certain amount of sea sand. It will not always stand a holdfast, but will frequently bear the weight of a recovery vehicle. The top surface of a salting is likely to prove treacherous, since the shorter turf or aquatic plants which cover the underlying beds of clay or loam are liable to abrade with very little effort, thereby exposing the soft and more readily yielding mass below.

A typical dry hinterland is depicted in Fig. 16.

(d) **Beaches**

(1) GENERAL.—A beach is the area or zone between the low tide and high tide shore lines. At some point landwards of the latter is the coast line proper, which may be an almost inconspicuous slope, a system of sand dunes, or an escarpment hundreds of feet in height.

The *extent* of a beach depends upon two main factors:
  (i) The amount by which the sea rises and falls.
  (ii) The slope of the beach.

If, for instance, the average difference in sea levels at high and low tide respectively is 10 ft. and the average slope seaward is 5°, a distance of 115 ft. of beach will be uncovered at low tide. The average beach slope is frequently much less than 5°, consequently many hundreds of yards may be uncovered at low tide.

(2) TIDES.—As tides ebb and flow in approximately 12 hours (to be explained in more detail later), the incoming tide will require about 6 hours to reach its maximum height, but if the slope of the beach is slight, the advance of the tide may occur with appreciable velocity. Hence it follows that a lack of knowledge of tide times and local conditions may have serious consequences on any recovery operation which may be in progress at the time of a flowing (i.e., rising) tide.

It is common knowledge that tidal motion is caused by the attraction of the moon, but if this were the only factor, the rise and fall of the water would be almost exactly the same *in amount* throughout the year at any given spot.

There are, however, two factors which affect this amount, viz. the variation in the distance between the earth and the moon, also the presence of the sun, which exerts an influence—though to a minor degree.

It follows, therefore, that when the moon and the sun are acting together, i.e. *when the sun, earth and moon are in line,* the total attraction must be at its *maximum,* hence what are called " *spring tides* " will result.

When the pull of the sun is at an angle to that of the moon, the total attraction is correspondingly reduced, and when the angle has reached 90° (i.e. when the moon is " in quadrature " with the sun), the combined pull is a *minimum* and what are known as the " *neap tides* " occur.

A little thought will show that *spring tides* occur at periods of the *full and new moon* and *neap tides* when the moon is in its *first and second quarters.*

The earth rotates on its axis once every 24 hours, but the moon requires 24 hours 48 minutes approx. to circle the earth. If tides were caused by the sun alone they would not only be much less marked, but they would occur at exactly the same *time* every day at any particular spot on the surface of the earth. The influence of the moon, however, is so much greater than that of the sun that the time of the tides depends largely upon the motion of the moon, viz. approximately 48 minutes *later* each day (actually 48 minutes 44 seconds); two high and two low tides therefore occur daily.

All these facts are carefully tabulated for marine use in the form of " Tide Tables ", which show the time of high and low water at any desired point. As previously pointed out, however, local conditions vary widely and details given in tabular form must be supplemented by observations or as the result of conversation with a person possessing special knowledge of the locality. *(Note:* this is of *particular* importance in connection with creeks and the estuaries of rivers).

Fig. 17

(3) WAVES.—The combination of tide and wave action has caused many important changes in the configuration of the coast line; this is particularly true of the action of the waves, which is both powerful and violent.

In so far as beaches are concerned, the undulatory wave—such as is met with out to sea—has no effect; it is only when such waves approach the shore and form " breakers " that their destructive energy is released. The effects are twofold: the first occurs when the wave, which may be several feet in height, curls over and the crest descends with a force partly gravitational and partly kinetic upon whatever happens to lie beneath; the second is due to the surf caused by the breaking-up of the wave, which carries forward rocks, stones, pebbles and sand in its passage up the beach. The latter action is intensified as the kinetic energy of the surf carries it well beyond the immediate sea level, after which the water—as soon as its stored energy is exhausted—surges back again. The actual breaking of the waves produces a succession of blows which are capable, in time, of disintegrating almost anything which may lie beneath them. The surf, in carrying backwards and forwards the material of which the beach is composed, causes a violent rubbing action to take place between the component parts as the result of which rocks become pebbles and pebbles sand in the course of time.

The importance of recovering a beach casualty without loss of time is obvious from a consideration of the above particulars. Not only will a vehicle or craft be subjected to wave blows and attrition if the sea is rough, but each succeeding wave may raise it bodily and drop it again upon the shore with

Fig. 18

sufficient violence to cause either its ultimate destruction or sufficiently serious damage to render it temporarily unusable, although the surface beneath may be smooth and only moderately hard.

Beach surfaces

SAND.—Sand will be found at any point where the disintegration of larger shells or stones has proceeded sufficiently far and where the waves are not so violent as to wash away the small particles as they form. Hence a sandy beach is normally of *gentle slope*. As the slope becomes steeper the size of the particles tends towards coarse grit and finally to what is known as " pea-shingle." Gently sloping sandy beaches provide large areas which are exposed at low tide, and since such sand is constantly being wetted and re-packed at each tide, it forms (in general) a good surface for tracked or wheeled vehicles. See Fig. 17.

An impression of recovery in progress on the sandy banks of a river in the tropics is given in Fig. 18.

Sand, however, is by no means the smallest particle met with on beach surfaces, since at their limit the sandy deposits of shallow water graduate down into muds and the only essential difference between the two classes is the state of division of the material.

Fig. 19

A very common type of sediment is one which is formed by the compression and partial drying of mud (i.e. clay). Much of the clay lying at the sea-shore is carried out to sea and deposited on the sea bed near the coast, but some may remain below the surface of the sand in patches, with occasional outcrops of moderate area. Either condition may lead to trouble, as if the soft wet clay becomes exposed (or is already exposed), it forms a treacherous surface requiring careful and skilled driving to negotiate.

SAND DUNES (Dry sand).—Wind-blown sands occur at various places along practically all sea coasts. Where broad tracts of sand are exposed at high tide (and particularly where the coast line has extended seawards, leaving stretches of dried-out sand), the prevailing winds carry the more finely divided material and heap it up into hills or dunes of irregular outline near to the shore. Such dunes often attain a height of around 150 ft., although elsewhere they form undulating sandy or grassy tracts. Fig. 19 shows a typical example of the seaward side of a dune area and indicates the kind of surface to be anticipated where the beach ends and the dunes begin.

As a general rule, sand dunes contain enough calcareous matter (pulverised sea shells) to support coarse grasses and sedges which tend to bind the loose sand together and hinder drifting. These growths, however, have little or no effect on the passage of wheeled or tracked vehicles.

Where there is nothing to bind the sand together, the surface becomes loose and mobile (generally as seen in Fig. 9), and the wheels of vehicles without

Fig 20

special provisions consequently dig themselves in and tractive effort falls to zero.

When, however, the surface of tyre or track in contact with the sand is large, wind-blown sand may be negotiated without too much difficulty. Tyre pressures must be lowered to the recommended figures for such work (see D.M.E. Technical Instruction No. B.400 and subsequent amendments), and after the passage of such a sandy area, immediately re-inflated.

The majority of tracked vehicles will tackle slopes up to 35° without much difficulty—particularly when fitted with wide tracks capable of "trapping" the loose sand. Skid turns are to be avoided, especially on slopes, and *all* turns on this kind of surface must be made with care.

No time should be wasted in an attempt to lay down a surface type of holdfast in wind-blown sand, but a baulk holdfast may be successfully employed.

SHINGLE AND PEBBLE BEDS.—Under this heading are included all beach deposits which consist of rounded stones which have been subjected to

Fig 21.

tide and wave action in the manner already described. Shingle beaches are frequently of great extent and may form a serious barrier to the passage of vehicles—particularly when the slope is considerable. In the case of

Fig. 22

wheeled vehicles the pebbles tend to roll under the tyres in a manner similar to the action of a ball bearing, and although a tracked vehicle suffers less in this respect, the stones are liable to become jammed between tracks and sprockets and cause stoppage of the vehicle even if no more serious damage is occasioned. Fig. 20 shows a representative shingle beach, whilst Fig. 21 depicts a stretch of large Kidney Stones (or " Cobbles" as they are called in some localities). Fig. 22 shows how shingle or pebble beds may be intermingled with sandy deposits, when the characteristics (from a vehicular point of view), become a combination of both the constituent surfaces.

QUICKSANDS.—Wherever a mixture of sand and water is maintained in certain proportions, a quicksand will result. This dangerous feature of a sea beach may be caused by a spring below the sand which, flowing upwards, is able to support down-flowing grains in equilibrium, or, as is more usually the case, a mixture of sand and water is left in a clay-bottomed hollow by the receding tide and, as the water is unable to pass through the dense clay bed, the sand is maintained in a " plastic " or semi-fluid condition. As previously mentioned, sand will eventually be ground down until it becomes clay and not all of this is washed out to sea, consequently, where outcrops of clay are found or where sub-strata of clay are evidenced, quicksands of greater or less extent may be expected to occur. THEY MUST BE AVOIDED as they are incapable of supporting *any* weight and will, on the contrary, engulf any vehicle or person attempting to cross them.

As a quicksand is merely a *condition* and does not require any particular kind of sand for its formation, it is usually difficult to distinguish from its surroundings apart from the fact that it is *absolutely flat and smooth*—even the fact that it is extremely wet is not immediately discernible.

(e) **Snow and ice**

Whilst the character of snow varies considerably with temperature, that of ice changes little—apart from the fact that it may be either smooth or rough and uneven, according to the nature of its formation.

At low temperatures—that is to say, from about 20° F, downwards— snow resembles very fine wind-blown sand except that it will readily pack under pressure. Above the temperature mentioned, snow becomes rather wet and will pack under the slightest pressure, whilst around freezing point (32° F.) it becomes slushy.

For *any* snow conditions wheeled vehicles must be provided with Chains, Overall or Chains Non-skid, as these will always improve traction and give some measure of grip and security on the fozen or ice-covered surfaces. For full details of these chains, see the appropriate Section—Appliances, Part I, " Chains, Overall and Chains Non-Skid ".

Tracked vehicles can proceed over snow and ice surfaces without undue difficulty in so far as traction is concerned, but care must be exercised

Fig. 23

when making turns. Moreover, on running into a deep drift of soft snow, this will very quickly pack in front so tightly that further progress becomes impossible.

If nothing in the nature of a snow plough is available, tightly packed snow must be dug away in order to render possible the free movement of both wheeled and tracked vehicles—see Fig. 23, which gives an indication of the extent to which such operations were necessary during the Italian campaign (early 1944).

www.ingramcontent.com/pod-product-compliance
Lightning Source LLC
Chambersburg PA
CBHW040312050426
42450CB00020B/3467